KU-516-273

Career Girls

Career Girls

Cautionary Tales for the Working Woman

Ms T. McGill

◻ SQUARE PEG

1 3 5 7 9 10 8 6 4 2

Square Peg, an imprint of Vintage,
20 Vauxhall Bridge Road,
London SW1V 2SA

Square Peg is part of the Penguin Random House group of companies whose
addresses can be found at global.penguinrandomhouse.com.

Penguin
Random House
UK

First published by Square Peg in 2018

Penguin.co.uk/vintage

A CIP catalogue record for this book is available from the British Library

ISBN 9781910931929

Design and typesetting by Dan Mogford
Illustrations copyright © Jennifer Dionisio 2018

Printed and bound by C&C Offset Printing Co., Ltd.

Penguin Random House is committed to a sustainable future for our business, our
readers and our planet. This book is made from Forest Stewardship Council®
certified paper.

MIX
Paper from
responsible sources
FSC® C018179

'I want every little girl who's told she's bossy, to be told instead she has leadership skills.'

Sheryl Sandberg

'We have to remember what's important in life: friends, waffles and work. Or waffles, friends, work. But work has to come third.'

Leslie Knope

Contents

A News Chronicle Publication   May 1951

Office Girl

NINEPENCE

£2,000 CONTEST FOR OFFICE GIRLS: *See page 18*

Introduction

'Give every girl an adequate number of rest periods during the day. Companies that are already using large numbers of women stress the fact that you have to make some allowances for feminine psychology. A girl has more confidence and consequently is more efficient if she can keep her hair tidied, apply fresh lipstick and wash her hands several times a day.'

'Eleven Tips on Getting More Efficiency Out of Women Employees', *Mass Transportation Magazine*, 1943

When I am not stuck in the bathroom tidying my hair, reapplying my lipstick and relentlessly washing my hands like Lady Macbeth, I am busy killing it at work. Nowadays women are just as common in the strip-lit, PC-ridden, be-cubicled habitat of the office as men and they are no longer solely confined to taking dictation, taking orders for lunch, and taking a pat on the arse with good humour. But how far have we truly come?

The current dictionary definition of 'career girl' is 'a woman whose main priority in life is achieving success in her career or profession'. It's hard not to hear the implication that a woman's *main* priority should really be something else, their personal life perhaps, or washing up, or their kids (the 'most important job in the world!') Despite the longevity of the assumption that men can manage a home life and a work life but women somehow cannot (too emotional? not enough upper-body strength?), the overwhelming majority of women persist in working. Even those who get married usually carry on – something that was practically illegal not so long ago. (This is what 'the marriage bar' refers to – rather than the place to get your prosecco and chocolate fondue at a wedding.)

So much has changed for the better – equal pay legislation, female CEOs, parental leave – but sadly there are still many everyday events, taking place in offices right now, which frustrate and diminish women in an unamusingly retro style. Professional women are still treated with more than a soupçon of suspicion: assertive = bitch, laidback = indecisive. Men are never asked how they manage the 'work-life balance', and why is it that women still have to organise the Christmas party?

This is what inspired me to draw together some of the irritations and challenges modern-day women face at work, accompanied by vintage-style illustrations and authentic advice from yesteryear. I can't promise this book will change your daily battles against the patriarchal set-up of the standard workplace, but it will reassure you that your frustrating experiences are shared by many, and that things are still improving. Stick together sisters – big up the achievements of other women you work with, as well as your own… and at the very least I encourage you to pester HR to make the AC a bit less sexist (air conditioning in the majority of offices is set to be comfortable for men's body temperatures rather than women's, FFS).

So if you're reading this as you drink your morning coffee, before you put your trainers in your bag and get your work shoes on to face the day, remember – the office is yours to command. As working-mother-of-three, Ms B. Knowles-Carter, says 'Power's not given to you. You have to take it.'

Ms T. McGill

Equal Pay

'A lot of girls are mesmerized by the glamour of a job. They think life would be wonderful as a model girl or a film star. To have something to do with ponies.'

A Young Girl's Guide to Intelligent Living,
Dora Shackell, 1964

There is a fraught atmosphere at Monday's board meeting when the gender pay gap figures are announced.

Thinking on his feet, Colz suggests a one-off bonus as reparation for the tampon tax for all qualifying employees. This idea gets kicked around for a while until several attendees get grossed out by the idea of periods. If only women were a bit more courageous about asking for payrises in the first place this wouldn't have turned into such a problem.

Colz's team think-wok some creative solutions to make the workplace more female-friendly. Given they can't alter the fact that, on average, women are paid 18.4% less than men – that's just life – perhaps the staff café could give women a special 18.4% discount on fruit, since they seem to like it so much? Colz has even put together a quite humorous PowerPoint about his thoughts.

Afterwards, Colz wishes 'the girls' could be a bit nicer about the efforts he's making. It's hard to be their champion when they're, to be frank, so ungrateful.

Ted Bulstrode doesn't trust anything that doesn't wear brogues. He tells Colz that he doesn't want to give the ladies too much responsibility because no one benefits if work becomes too stressful for them...and anyway most of them would prefer to be at home looking after their children, rather than paying some other poor cow to do it. It's the kids he feels sorry for.

No one has ever seen Mrs Bulstrode in person but in photos of the two of them together at trade events, she has the tight-lipped expression of a shamed MP's wife 'standing by him' at a press briefing.

Ted's assistant, Emily, is twenty-two years old. She's just discovered that the gender pay gap is currently estimated to close in 2117.

She's psyched that her great-great-grand daughter is going to witness this momentous step forward for the sisterhood. She's made herself a tick-off calendar that she intends to hand down the maternal line.

Emily's best work-mate, Sal, has just been through the somewhat humiliating experience of announcing to the office that she's pregnant.

When she told Ted, he said 'Well, that's that then', which she found rather enigmatic. Colz was eager to let her know that he's discovered from his research as part of his 'Feminism Fetish' (his little joke) that she will be financially worse off than her nulliparous sisters now, particularly as she is 'ethnic'.

Emily has worked out a brilliant Robin Hood scheme to redress the pay gap.

She pretends to undertake a major sporting event every six months and harasses her co-workers into sponsoring her on a fake webpage which quietly refunds all the women who donate with an additional share of the revenue from their male colleagues.

This time she is swimming the Channel for 'equality'. No one yet has commented, beyond Ted asking her if she has to cover herself in whale fat.

Work/Life
Balance

'A social service meeting, an
afternoon tea, a matinee, a whatnot,
is no excuse for there being no
dinner ready when a husband comes
home from a hard day's work.'

Sex Satisfaction and Happy Marriage,
Reverend Alfred Henry Tyrer, 1951

Anna's boyfriend, Sid, can't do the washing up because he works from home and he has to have firm boundaries to his day.

Sid was made redundant from his job selling advertising space three months ago. He's starting up his own Social Media consultancy but he first needs to create a really cracking logo. As he has no design skills, it is taking Sid some time to action this.

It takes no time at all for Anna to action ordering a removal van for Sid and asking him to pack his things.

Anna is the only person in the office who knows that her colleague Charlotte has three children.

In the six years she has worked for the company Charlotte has managed to imply that she is dealing very bravely with a serious illness, which explains why she leaves before 7pm every day.

When Charlotte went on her honeymoon her husband locked her work phone in the hotel safe.

Under the guise of forgetting her book, her sunglasses and her comfy flipflops she managed to check her emails three times on the first day.

She was so distracted by a comment Nathan made about the June presentation that she has no memory of the welcome sundowners on the beach that her husband still talks about fondly.

Charlotte and Jess are having a friendly conversation in the playground, when they overhear their children talking about playdates.

Milly says 'Oh you won't be able to come to my house as Mum will be working'.

'Don't worry', Ruby replies kindly, 'You can always come to mine. My mum doesn't do anything at all'.

Charlotte and Jess both flush but neither knows which of them has come off worse.

Anna is glad to be out while Sid packs his stuff, but when she finds herself trying to engage her Tinder hook-up in conversation about the strengths and weaknesses of her company's key rival she realises she needs to take a holiday.

Her date is a very pleasant marine biologist but he doesn't have any insight at all into what would give them the competitive edge in China.

Anna has decided to read a pile of self-help books to 'redress the asymmetry of her work-life calibration'.

She now has a multicoloured A3 mindmap covered in phrases like 'more sleep', 'houseplants!', 'no more Haribo for lunch', 'retrain as librarian?', 'get shower fixed', 'friends or exercise?', and 'fake own death?'

Interacting with Colleagues

'Be tactful when issuing criticisms. Women are often sensitive; they can't just shrug off harsh words the way men do. Never ridicule a woman – it breaks her spirit.'

Mass Transportation Magazine, 1943

'Two espressos and a pain au raisin would be great', is how Fi's boss greets her when she arrives for the 9 o'clock meeting.

'And a flat white for me thanks Patrick', she says, giving him a dead-eyed smile and sitting down to peruse the agenda.

Bill Jenkins has been at the firm for 30 years and Patrick is extremely downcast when news emerges that Bill has been summarily dismissed for sexual harassment. The company is currently dealing with five separate lawsuits on the matter.

After Bill has been escorted from the premises, some of his department gather in Patrick's office to commiserate. He was apparently a 'really good guy' as well as a 'real laugh'.

After 'that thing with Bill', Patrick becomes increasingly nervous about his all-staff communications and asks Fi to read over every draft email in case there's anything 'the politically correct ones' might object to.

Fi reminds him that she's an Inventory Specialist rather than an HR Manager. However, she is the only woman on the team so Patrick says she 'has to take responsibility'. She excises his 'Sexual Harassment Prevention' brainwave whereby female staff are instructed to submit lists of male colleagues they are prepared to hug.

On her Health-and-Safety-recommended hourly screen breaks, Fi stares into the middle distance and thinks about breaking both of Ben's legs.

She shares a cubicle with him but they never speak to one another. He refers to himself as 'Benjy' or 'the Benster', signs off emails with 'Warmest', walks around in his socks, does not invest in high-quality earphones and eats a lot of tuna.

Sadly, after careful checking of the company code of conduct, Fi concludes none of these infractions are grounds for dismissal.

Fi soon regrets her decision to prove she can keep up with the lads after a late-nighter in All Bar One. Ben seems to think he now has an open invitation to stand too close to her in the coffee room and squeeze her shoulders in a matey manner when he walks past her chair.

Eventually she is forced to use 'feminist eyes' on him. He stops calling her 'Fun Fi' and refers to her as 'the ice bitch' behind her back from this point on.

B en seems alarmed when it transpires that Lauren has been assigned his IT helpdesk call. 'Normally Roy comes...' he murmurs as she starts to investigate what's caused the 57 gaudy pop-up porn windows to infect his desktop.

The five minutes it takes Lauren to fix the problem are very quiet: the hush only punctuated by the sound of Fi typing away at the desk opposite, an expression of great concentration on her face.

'Just watch your Google searches...' Lauren says casually as she leaves, catching Fi's eye. Fi considers this an excellent Tuesday.

Leadership

'There may be many successful and
happily married women doctors,
lawyers, artists, musicians, writers,
and the like, but I believe that being
the wife of an executive is a full-
time job in itself.'

Good Housekeeping, 1956

Scott has selected Narinder to go on a week-long exclusive leadership course in the Brecon Beacons.

Narinder starts to say that she's really pleased to have had her contribution recognised when Scott interrupts her with 'it looks good for the division not to be sending another bloke'.

Jen was a quietly authoritative, well-liked manager when she was sent on the previous incarnation of Narinder's course – the 'Candour Combat Convention'.

Jen's Assistant, Jacob, now visibly winces whenever she asks him for the '360 degree kill chain' on their seasonal strategic proposals, or the 'blood trail' on the analysis charts she is unimpressed with.

When it turns out that there has been a significant error in the data analysis for their biggest client, Scott decides it's a perfect opportunity for Narinder to practise her leadership skills. Scott has been handling the top-level meetings with Herr Grossekatze in Munich thus far but he thinks Narinder should book herself a flight over there ay-sap.

Narinder thanks Scott for his trust in her, then reminds him that she's leaving for the 'Thought Intrapreneurs of Tomorrow' course this afternoon so sadly she'll have to pass.

Narinder has been on the 'Thought Intrapreneurs of Tomorrow' course for three days now and is becoming increasingly confused.

The dawn mindfulness sessions are relaxing but she felt a tension between her and Brad after she questioned his arrangement of the logs during the raft-building exercise.

This afternoon she has been asked to paint her leadership style. At the moment all she is able to produce are spiralling grey circles.

A scandal erupts on day five of the course when Brad starts talking about his wife's relationship with his brother during the trust exercise. Nobody knows exactly what to say when he starts throwing the beanbags at the Nespresso machine and sobbing.

Narinder takes Brad for a breath of fresh air. He is soon feeling calmer and they agree that neither of them are sorry to have missed the next exercise. They will never know what their 'Business Spirit Animal' is, and what it might be like to express this through dance, but they can live with that.

On day six of the course, the tenor changes from mindfulness and massages to something rather more aggressive.

Narinder is blindfolded and put in the back of a van at 5am. After being driven for what feels like miles she is released and instructed to make her own way back to the hotel to demonstrate her initiative.

After taking five minutes to find the nearest road, Narinder calls a taxi. She is back in bed by 5.46.

Office Etiquette

'"I am a woman executive. Is it permissible for me to pick up the check for a male customer I am entertaining as a representative of our firm?"

If the bill is to be paid at the desk, quietly put money to cover it on the check and ask your customer to take care of it. Either leave the tip yourself or ask him to take care of it out of the change. Try to avoid passing any money yourself, for other diners in the restaurant would not necessarily understand the circumstances.'

Amy Vanderbilt's New Complete Book of Etiquette, 1952

Kelly has noticed that Colz seems to speak to her in a different way than he does to her other co-workers.

When he ends a conversation with 'innit' she realises that it's either her age, her class or her colour that is freaking him out.

Perhaps he is, in fact, a victim of her intersectionality?

Colz is a 'cool boss' who holds regular after-work bowling and karaoke sessions. He's really disappointed that 'the Kellinator' doesn't seem to think it's important to attend. After all, Si even has kids and he still manages to make it every time.

Kelly cannot summon the energy to explain to Colin that Si can afford to get a cab, and doesn't have to change into running shoes and use his keys as a knuckle-duster in order to feel even slightly safe on his walk home from the bus stop.

While they wait for the final printouts for the forecasting meeting, the working group enjoys a bit of chitchat. Colz says that Kelly's hair looks fancy today.

Kelly is perplexed by this as Emily, sitting next to her, is wearing a glittery unicorn headband.

Everyone thinks Emily is a sweet but completely useless airhead. Her desk is covered in pictures of cartoon llamas and she opens her eyes really widely and pauses for a long time whenever anyone asks her a question.

Emily is actually a passive-aggressive genius who has worked out that this is the best way to maximise her work-to-pay ratio. She is biding her time like a cute, lazy shark lurking at the bottom of a reef of naïve clown fish.

The kitchen on the third floor has become a biohazardous area.

Pamela used to clean everything up at the end of the day but one Tuesday when Colz passed her his dirty coffee cup she just snapped.

Pamela has been Communications Director for seven years.

Colz mentions to Kelly that 'someone needs to sort the kitchen out', a month after Pamela resigns from her honorary position of chief bottle-washer.

Kelly has always hated Pamela, and called her a humourless martyr behind her back, but when their eyes meet over the printer a profound connection is made. Over the next few months they send each other emails speculating on what new life forms might be evolving on the tea towels.

Securing
a Promotion

'Women will not require increases
related to length of service as they will
retire for the purpose of getting married
as soon as they get the chance.'

Postmaster General, 1869

Pamela has recently been headhunted by a rival firm.

At the next board meeting Ted spends some time discussing the 'lack of commitment' he has observed in female colleagues and even uses the word 'traitor' at one particularly emotive moment.

However, they somehow manage to find funds for the payrise and promotion that they could in no way countenance when Pamela asked for them a month previously.

Pamela has been given a fancy new job description and office, thanks to her promotion. Her title is Senior Vice President and Director of Strategic Messaging and Culture which requires some delicate typesetting to fit on her business cards.

Pamela is amused to discover that her new office has a skylight which means that she now has a literal glass ceiling to remind her how far she has come.

Fi's mum has read an article that claims women only apply for jobs when they are sure they are 100% qualified, whereas men go for them when they meet 60% of the criteria.

Fi is moved to reformat her CV, removing her swimming awards and Piano Grade 3 from it. She puts herself forward for a promotion.

When she checks the job description she realises that she has actually been 100% qualified for this new role for over three years.

Patrick explains that Fi has been unsuccessful in her application in this instance.

Nathan just came across as more of a team player and a more natural fit for the client base. The golf guys can get a bit edgy around vaginas. (Patrick doesn't use these exact words but his meaning is clear).

Fi summons up the courage to ask Patrick if she can take him to lunch to get his advice on moving up the corporate ladder. Patrick has many words of wisdom for her, which he shares generously over steak.

Fi should 'man up' and 'thrust' herself forward more; have 'the balls' to own and communicate her successes; and stop 'acting like Cinderella' and 'nail' her networking skills.

He also suggests trying to avoid wasting time on getting to know junior members of the team. 'Pamela even gets her team birthday cards!' he snorts incredulously.

When Fi is interviewed by Ted for a senior position in his division he is very impressed with her CV. His one concern is about her five-year plan, given she is in her early thirties. He impresses upon her that the company invests a lot in training its staff and they expect a great deal of commitment in return.

In her second-round interview, Fi wears more lipstick than usual, laughs at all Ted's jokes about Excel and manages to express a deep distaste for children as part of her answer about what makes their company a leader in the field. She gets the job.

Dressing
for Work

'From my own experience, a low ebb
of energy can also lead to a sudden
feeling of despair when I open the
wardrobe door. When this happens,
I try to forget about what I'm going
to wear for a few minutes and lie
down with my feet elevated.'

How To Be a Well-Dressed Wife,
Anne Fogarty, 1959

Emily felt confident when she left home this morning that she was projecting her personal brand through her outfit, but given the bewilderment on Ted's face, perhaps the hand-knitted pussy hat, tulle-ballerina-skirt-with-blazer-combo and neon DMs are a step too far.

She assumes Ted is making a mental note to never take her seriously, but equally he could just be feeling sad and embarrassed about his boring navy suit.

In a rather tense meeting about the dress code for the firm, Ted tells Emily that heeled court shoes are the preferred option for female employees. Emily is confident that all her shoes have heels so unfortunately Ted is led onto a circuitous explanation of why high-heeled shoes just look somehow more professional.

Emily is also very game for a conversation about what constitutes 'professional'.
In the end they come to an unspoken agreement that Emily has a chiropodial-political problem which gives her special dispensation to wear flats.

Colz has implemented Casual Clothes Friday in his department as a policy to show the 'human' and 'relaxed' face of the corporation. He likes to call it 'Fierce Fashion Friday' to make it more aspirational.

Colz cannot wait to show off the hilarious socks his brother got him for Christmas. Even he doesn't know if he likes them in an ironic or unironic way but who cares, they have crazy giraffes on them, and giraffes feel very now.

By week two Colz is moved to draw up a twelve-point guide to clarify what 'casual' actually means, and what staff, as flagbearers of corporate identity, need to bear in mind. Every. Single. Day. Of. The. Week.

He's not naming names of course, but everyone knows it's because of Si's overreaction to being told he can't wear shorts, and definitely not short shorts.

Si wonders if he's able to raise it with HR as an example of sexual discrimination.

'Nailed it' Charlotte thinks as she wraps up her webinar on how nanodegrees can help expand her colleagues' skill set.

Her high is slightly crushed when Si points out a brown smear on her shirt, which is either her son's poo or the chocolate spread he ate out of the jar for breakfast this morning.

She's confident it is the latter but decides against further investigation.

The following day, Charlotte moves a clothes rail into the office.

In the ensuing weeks, her work wardrobe evolves. First she acquires a pale cream overcoat. Then she brings in all her nice shoes from home to keep them 'safe'.

Anna sometimes finds her gazing in deep contemplation at her new handbag, while 'looking over some urgent reports' that unfortunately require her to miss her little ones' bathtime.

Making
the Most of
Meetings

'No doubt you have heard of the
secretary who in her efficiency
fairly scolds her boss as though he
were her erring child. Privileged
employees, because of long years of
service of inestimable value to their
employers, may be permitted such
idiosyncrasies; but, as a beginner,
no such privileges are in store for
you. Young people who are not
cheerful are too easy to replace.'

Fitting Yourself for Business,
Elizabeth Gregg MacGibbon, 1941

Fi's mother has recently read an article in *Forbes Magazine* which points out that men interrupt 33% more often when they are talking to women in meetings. She has been preparing to finally take on Airtime Alan by practising breath control in the local pool so that he can no longer use her inhalations as openings.

After a few failed interceptions, he finally manages to launch into his usual 'That's all very well but…' only to find that Fi has raised a warning finger at him and continued to speak, increasingly loudly, until he is forced to give up. When Fi finishes her point, Kelly accidentally starts clapping.

Pamela responds strongly to Alan's brazen bropropriation of her game-changing idea for corporate responsibility. Afterwards, Penny from HR asks if she needs some time away from the office environment, perhaps for an anger management course?

Next time, when Alan rephrases her idea and claims it as his own, instead of gritting her teeth and hissing 'Yes, Alan, exactly what I just said', Pamela smiles sweetly and thanks him for explaining her idea so clearly.

Alan looks genuinely delighted with her praise.

Initially, Kelly feels an intoxicating mix of excitement and nerves when Si asks for her help with preparing the annual presentation to the board. For the first time in months she doesn't have her dream about being stuck in a lift that's on fire, which she assumes represents her feelings about her career.

At their first brainstorming session, Si gifts her the catering forms and asks her to check the attendees' dietary requirements.

There's a flurry of panicked but hushed activity when Si's PowerPoint fails to load properly. After twenty-five minutes Pamela raises her voice over the hubbub to suggest they reschedule for the next day. Ben says 'All right, Mum!' in a jokey tone but it falls somewhat flat.

Unfortunately Si and Patrick have a client lunch that is likely to take up most of the next afternoon. After a further twenty minutes of schedule negotiation a new time is agreed.

As they leave the conference room, Emily takes out her headphones and checks with Kelly that they did indeed just have a meeting about having a meeting.

At their introductory mentoring session Narinder joins Sandra sitting peacefully in her gorgeous sea-frost-painted corner office.

Sandra has been CEO for fifteen years now. She smiles as she shows Narinder a recent press article digging up the old rumour that in the 1980s she fired her entire Marketing team on Christmas Eve by fax from the labour ward after giving birth to her twins.

Narinder can't figure out if she's to take this as inspiration or as a warning.

Sandra thought she'd successfully kept her impending 'big birthday' quiet but when cake emerges with a card full of witty messages from people she barely knows, she realises she has been rumbled.

When Colz makes a joke about how they need to introduce a 'safe cry space' now she's reached 'that time of her life', Sandra silently wonders to herself if a safe rage room might be more appropriate.

Office Romance

'A woman's sexual response is so
general and diffuse that frequently
she does not even know that she
is being aroused, and even more
frequently is quite unaware that
her behaviour is arousing the boy
beyond the boundaries which she
herself would wish to maintain.'

When You Marry, Evelyn Duvall
and Reuben Hill, 1953

Lauren is very comfortable in her sexuality and hasn't felt it necessary to announce to the office that she leads a blissfully happy domestic life with her girlfriend Bea. But when Si starts showing her pictures of him participating in last year's Tough Mudder and complaining about his wife, she feels moved to gently explain her situation.

A look of horror flashes briefly over Si's face, but he masks it gamely, clapping her on the back and calling her a dark horse. Over the next week he tries to engage Lauren in discussion about how hot Anna from Business Development is.

In the post-#metoo climate, management feels twitchy about what constitutes sexual harassment and what's just 'Si's bantz', so self-appointed expert Colz calls a meeting with Penny from HR to 'thrash it out'. In a totally non-violent or sexual way of course.

After weeks of flirty emails, blushing at the watercooler and bedroom eyes in the breakout area, Ben and Anna finally go out for a drink.

Anna wouldn't usually consider a second date with a grown man who has a poster of Tiger Woods on his wall, but his flat is closer to the office than hers so she gives it another few goes.

Ben is dismayed when Anna tells him she doesn't want to take their relationship 'to the next level', and snatches the poetry he's printed out for her off her desk. Later he has a surprisingly deep conversation with Colz about the twenty-first century's crisis of masculinity.

Ben seems unexpectedly nervous before his presentation at the budget reforecast meeting but Colz whispers, 'You got this buddy'.

When Anna questions the figure that's been assigned to her department, Ben's voice rises an octave and he embarks on a long monologue about 'statistical post-processing' which veers into some dark places no one in the room quite understands.

Anna vows never to sleep with a colleague again.

S andra has been dreading this meeting. Redundancy processes are always hard but Scott has been with the company a long time and won't be expecting it. She's asked Penny from HR to wait outside, until called in to go through the generous package details.

Scott enters the room buoyantly until he notices with alarm the way Sandra is clenching her stressball.

As expected, Scott shouts a lot and refuses to listen to Sandra's explanation of impartiality and being led by the numbers. However by the time Penny comes in he has calmed down somewhat.

He's no longer threatening to cancel their summer holiday and has even agreed to pick up some olive oil on the way home as they've run out and Sandra won't be back until late. Once again, Sandra is reminded of the dangers of mixing the personal with the professional.

"Meet our new star," Hugh cried,
raising her arm, "Sultrie Shaw!"

The Office Christmas Party

'It is always permissible to ask
a hostess if you may "bring" a
dancing man who is a stranger to
her. It is rather difficult to ask for
an invitation for an extra girl, and
still more difficult to ask for older
people, because the hostess has no
ground on which she can refuse
without being rude.'

Etiquette, Emily Post, 1922

It's been a demoralising year for Si's department and he's been asked to 'apply some thought to headcount'. 'That's why we need the party to end all parties,' he explains to his PA Jackie, 'It's all about transmitting an attitude of success'.

Si has been in competition with Colz for the last four years for the title of 'Best Bash Boss'. It's four-nil to Colz so far. Si wishes he knew where Colz found that mixologist who made those cool cocktails that looked like lava lamps.

Jackie's calendar already looked like 'The Battle of the Bastards' sequence in *Game of Thrones* and now she has Si's party to sort out.

She has forgotten the kids' PE kit three times this month, is thinking about gin and tonics before 5pm on a regular basis, and desperately needs a haircut. The other day she considered having the cat put down to remove one of the practical and emotional drains on her energy.

In late November Si calls Jackie in to his office to check progress on 'his jamboree' as he's taken to calling it.

Jackie runs him through the list of high-end activities she has booked… a sushi bar, casino tables, boutique goody bags that support local charities. 'Great', says Si, 'But what about the vodka luge?' When he looks over the budget he gets Jackie to cancel the goody bags.

Everyone agrees Ben is a solid 6 in a good light but after the vodka has been flowing for a few hours, Narinder distinctly hears one of her colleagues telling him his new beard makes him look like Jake Gyllenhaal.

B rad has sunk four too many Aperol Spritzes and decided now is the time to talk to the CEO about his visionary plans for the company's future.

Narinder knows he is committing professional suicide but decides to hang back and enjoy listening to him talk Sandra through all the mistakes she's made. It turns out he's really keen to be 'upfront' and 'call a spade a spade' despite the 'clear sexual tension' he feels between them.

A queasy hush hangs over the floor the morning after the Christmas do. Jacob can't remember who he ended up with in the only loo with a lock on it, Narinder recalls with a pang of shame being sick on the night-bus, and Brad's desk has been cleared.

Si is pleased, certain that this year he's beaten Colz to the party crown. He's heard that Data Analysis's festivities ended at 10.30pm and Colz was kicked out of 'spoons for bad behaviour.

Jackie feels a heavy sense of deja-vu as she manhandles the vodka luge off her desk and opens the spreadsheet to make a start on next year's celebrations.

Acknowledgements

No man is an island. And neither is this woman.
For making all my teamwork dreams come true thanks go
to: Editor extraordinaire Victoria Murray-Browne,
Charlotte Humphery, Rowan Yapp, Clara Farmer,
Rowena Skelton-Wallace, Jennifer Dionisio, Shabana Cho,
Jane Kirby, Sam Coates, Monique Corless, Penny Liechti,
Tom Drake-Lee, Christina Ellicott, Christina Usher,
Lily Buckmaster, David Heath, Mia Quibell-Smith,
Candice Carty-Williams, Gemma Avery, Emma Buttle-
Smith, Maddy Hartley and Dan Mogford.

Picture credits